St John Southworth

Priest and Martyr

by
Fr Michael Archer

Taken from the CTS Pamphlet by Godfrey Anstruther, O.P.
and the book of the same name by E.E.Reynolds

Dedicated to the memory of the late Godfrey Anstruther, O.P.
who did so much to further the cause
of the English and Welsh Martyrs

*All booklets are published thanks to the
generous support of the members of the
Catholic Truth Society*

CATHOLIC TRUTH SOCIETY
PUBLISHERS TO THE HOLY SEE

Contents

Poor Persecuted Catholics

The England into which John Southworth was born in the year 1592, in the county of Lancashire, during the reign of Elizabeth I, was a land where the Catholic faith was under constant attack. In 1558 the Catholic bishops of the Catholic Queen Mary's reign were deposed and replaced by Protestant bishops. Parliament with The Act of Supremacy in 1559 made it High Treason to maintain the Pope's authority, and imposed an oath acknowledging the Queen as Supreme Governor in all spiritual or ecclesiastical things as well as temporal.

At the same time the Book of Common Prayer from King Edward VI's time was ordered to replace the Catholic Missals and Catholic prayer books. The Mass was prohibited, attendance at the Protestant services was compulsory. Even at the beginning of Elizabeth's reign there was the death sentence for declaring the Pope to be the head of the Church of Christ. The fines for non-attendance at Church were the equivalent of four days' wages. In 1571 Parliament imposed the Thirty Nine Articles as defining the beliefs of this new Church of England, printed to this day in every copy of the Book of Common Prayer, and declaring that the Catholic beliefs in the Mass were "blasphemous fables". To start with,

Parliament was more interested in making money with the heavy fines and confiscation of property, especially from the great Catholic landowners, than on hunting down Priests. The hope was that the Catholic faith would die with the passing of the old Priests from the reign of Queen Mary. But then began efforts on several fronts to restore the Catholic faith and even overturn the Protestant Monarchy and Parliament.

A catholic seminary in France

In 1568 a Catholic College, or Seminary, was established in Douai, a town in Northern France, to train Priests for the Catholic Church in England. The first of these Priests arrived secretly in 1574. The founder of this Seminary was William Allen, a fellow of Oriel College, Oxford, a fellow Lancastrian of John Southworth, and later to be made a Cardinal.

The northern rising

Then in 1569 a rebellion, the Northern Rising, occurred led by the Catholic Earls and gentry in an attempt to overturn the Government. Their armies posed a really serious threat to Elizabeth, but on reaching York they were defeated. Retribution was swift – 800 of the rebels were hanged, and 57 Nobles and Gentlemen had their estates confiscated. In York alone 28 Priests were hung, drawn and quartered, plus 11 laymen who had harboured

Priests in their homes. The plight of Catholics was then made even worse when Pope Pius V excommunicated Queen Elizabeth in 1570 and this increased the resolve of Parliament to regard all Catholics as potential traitors. In 1585 the Act against 'Jesuit, seminary Priests, and other such like disobedient persons' was passed declaring it to be High Treason for a Priest to be within the Queen's dominions, and that it was a felony for anyone to receive or relieve a Priest.

In 1587 Queen Elizabeth had Mary Queen of Scots beheaded because she was seen as a threat to the throne. Some Catholics regarded Catholic Mary Queen of Scots as the legitimate successor to the Catholic Queen Mary, Elizabeth being considered by Catholics to be the illegitimate daughter of Henry VIII and Anne Boleyn. On Elizabeth's death it was in fact Mary Queen of Scots' son James who became King of England and Scotland. As a child he had been taken away from his Catholic mother and brought up as a Protestant.

The Spanish Armada

The 'treacherous nature' of Catholics was 'proven' by the attempted invasion of England by King Philip of Spain, with promised subsidies from the Pope, in 1588, with his huge Armada fleet of ships, and colossal army waiting in the Netherlands to be transported across the Channel. Fortunately for Elizabeth the skill of her navy and the weather, and the lack of boats to transport the Spanish troops, prevented the invasion. But it had been a very close call. So it was no surprise that Acts were passed by Parliament to proscribe Catholicism as a threat to the very safety and existence of the State.

A faith in hiding

In 1593, the year after John Southworth's birth, the laws against Catholics were made even more drastic and imposed with much greater efficiency. By the end of her reign the law declared that a Priest or a convert was in fact a traitor. Even a hundred and fifty years later after Elizabeth's death, Lord Chief Justice Mansfield could say, 'according to the Penal Statutes of Queen Elizabeth, which are still in force, it is High Treason for a Priest to come into England'. By the end of Elizabeth's reign in 1603 there were 188 Catholic martyrs of whom 126 were Priests.

Apart from his own words on the scaffold at the end of his life that he was born in Lancashire, we know nothing of John Southworth's early history until he enters the English Seminary in Douai. However he would have been very conscious all his young life of the constant and frightening persecution of Catholics. His namesake in the same county, Sir John Southworth, an ardent Catholic was first imprisoned for his religion in 1568 and spent the greater part of the next twenty years in gaol. One of his sons, a Catholic Priest, was interned for ten years in Wisbech Castle. Originally Sir John owned some 14,000 acres, but by the end of the seventeenth century practically all had been lost by payment of fines, by supporting the Catholic cause, and through loyalty to the king during the civil wars.

In his early years John Southworth would have been familiar with reports of relatives and neighbours being fined and imprisoned. He must as a boy have learned the precautions that had to be taken to safeguard the Mass and to shelter the Priests who brought the Sacraments. The risks however were not so great as in London, for in Lancashire there was a very fervent and devout Catholic population. Remote farms and hamlets made it easier for the faith to be practised and for Priests to be concealed.

John Southworth was eleven years old when James I came to the throne in 1603. Despite hopes that James would lessen the burden of the Elizabethan penal enactments the first Parliament of his reign confirmed the Elizabethan statutes, and insisted on their enforcement. Sir Robert Cecil, Secretary of State, told the Venetian Ambassador that the purpose of the penal laws was to make it impossible to practise the Catholic religion in England.

The gunpowder plot and penal laws

In 1605 came the criminal folly of the Gunpowder Plot, by Catholic conspirators trying to blow up the House of

Parliament, and which therefore provided a perfect pretext for making the penal laws even more rigorous. John Southworth was then thirteen years old. The next year the Act of 1606 made it obligatory for every adult to attend the Parish Church and receive communion according to the Anglican Prayer Book; Catholics were to be excluded from Parliament, all public office, the army and the navy; inheritance of land was endangered, movement restricted, even the number of horses they could own was limited. Catholics were virtually a separate community without many of the rights of common citizenship. Fortunately for Catholics it was another matter to put these laws into effect with no national police force, and much depended on the local magistrate and local sentiment – loopholes abounded. But of course the laws were there and it only needed a jealous neighbour or informer for them to come into deadly effect.

Catholic education in secret and isolated secular priests

Catholic education had to be given in secret, and we don't know in what form John Southworth received his. There were little secret Catholic schools in Lancashire, so he may have attended one of these, or received private tuition at home from visiting priests. There were now no Catholic bishops in England. From 1599 to 1621

Archpriests were appointed by the Pope to oversee the mission, but their authority was too limited to be effective. Seminary Priests had very much to fend for themselves with family and friends to support and protect them.

Normally a priest is subject to his bishop, but in seventeenth-century England there was no Catholic bishop exercising full authority. When a young secular priest, fresh from one of the seminaries, landed in this country, he was to a great extent left to his own resources; there was no one in authority to whom he could look for guidance. If he went to his native part of the country, as many did, he would soon find his work; but on occasion a priest would arrive in London and have to find what shelter he could until he got in touch with Catholics. This lack of system in placing priests or of keeping in touch with them partly explains the absence of information about them. Martyrdoms were usually reported to Douay or one of the other seminaries, but these were limited to accounts of arrest, trial and death. As we shall see in following the ministry of John Southworth, there are completely blank periods as far as the records go. The priests themselves, though willing and eager to give their lives in defence of the Church, desired nothing better than to exercise their functions in obscurity. We must think of them carrying on their work without the fortifying guidance of a bishop, or the possibility of spiritual renewal in retreat, or even the company of other priests. It was a life that called for great self-discipline. It is a marvel that so many spent years of faithful ministry in such isolation, under the threat of being denounced, imprisoned, and put to death. It was by the quiet labours of such men that the Faith survived these long years of persecution.

It was during the reign of King James I and under these conditions that John Southworth as a young man aged twenty-one, and clearly posessed of a very fervent Catholic faith, left England for the Seminary in Douai in 1613.

Douay 1613 - 1619

A seminary producing 'happy seed'
for a 'barren land'; becoming a priest

In these pages the old spelling 'Douay' will be used for the Seminary as distinct from 'Douai', the town or university. Our first real piece of evidence about our martyr is an entry in the Douay College Diary under the date 4th July 1613 which reads in translation, 'John Southworth of Lancashire, here known as Lee, was received into the College as a convictor.' A convictor was a student who was supported by his family or friends. As a precaution against informers it was usual for students to assume another name. John was then twenty-one years of age. He would start his studies with a two year course of scholastic philosophy, and then four years study of theology. The College had a great reputation as can be gathered from the report of Dr Matthew Kellison, its President. This title of 'President' was in use until the Seminary's last move to Chelsea from Old Hall Green, Ware, Hertfordshire, in 1975. Dr Kellison wrote to the Papal Nuncio at Brussels as follows:

'From its first foundation (a period of fifty-four years) the seminary has sent to the English Mission nearly

1000 priests. Of these 111 have with constancy suffered holy martyrdom for the Catholic Faith and the dignity of the Apostolic See. Very many others, while bravely working on the English Mission, have either been taken by the persecutors and thrown into prison, or sent into exile, or else, worn out by great hardships and the filth of prison, have died in the confession of the same faith'.

Among John Southworth's fellow students were two future martyrs; Thomas Maxfield and Henry Morse. Maxfield left for the mission in July 1615 and had barely a year of active ministry before his arrest. In his last letter to Dr Kellison he wrote, 'I think myself most happy that I branched out of, and still remain a member of, that blessed House of Douay, that has afforded to our poor, barren country so much good and happy seed. I will never cease, God willing, to pray for you and my good and dearly beloved brethren, and for the prosperity of that House, both in life and after death.' He suffered at Tyburn (today's Marble Arch) on 1 July 1616. On the news of his martyrdom there was celebrated a Mass of thanksgiving and a solemn 'Te Deum', the Church's special hymn of thanksgiving and praise. One can only imagine the feelings and emotions that would have been felt by his fellow students, the staff and all connected with the College at such an occasion, which would have not, sadly, been too infrequent.

The second of the future martyrs was Henry Morse, three years younger than John Southworth. He was only at Douay for a short while before transferring to the English College in Rome and eventually entered the Society of Jesus, or the Jesuits as they are commonly known. But the two were to meet years later in plague-stricken London.

On 14th July 1614 John Southworth received the tonsure, the ceremony that made him officially a cleric. At the end of December 1615 he took the College Oath, a very solemn occasion and a big commitment - 'I swear to Almighty God that I have the prompt intention, so far as God's Grace shall help me, of receiving sacred orders in due time, and of returning to England to gain the souls of my neighbours, wherever it shall seem good in the Lord to the superior of this College, for the purpose of its institution, to order me to do so.' He suffered bouts of ill health, and had to return to England briefly to recuperate.

On his return to Douay plague broke out in the locality and the students were confined to the College. But despite these setbacks in September of 1617 he received the four Minor Orders in Cambrai from the Archbishop there. In the next year, again at Cambrai, he received the Major Orders from the Archbishop, subdiaconate and diaconate, on Easter Sunday 1618. There were still some more studies to be done, but at last the long hoped-for day arrived, and he was ordained a Priest on 13th December 1619.

The Douay Diary describes him offering up his first Mass "with deep feeling to his risen Lord." In the Douay College records we read, 'John Southworth (here known as Lee), alumnus (student) and priest of this College, with the usual faculties for the winning of souls, was chosen for the vineyard of England.' He was twenty-seven years old when he left Douay for England.

London 1619 - 1624

The mission - a time of trial

From 1599 to 1621 Archpriests were appointed by the Pope to supervise the mission but their authority was too limited to be effective. In the very year that John Southworth arrived in England, 1619, the Archpriest, William Harrison, gave his report on the Catholic situation at that time.

'With regard to our affairs, they are in the same state as usual. The pillaging of property, the squalor of prisons, the intimidations from magistrates, the raids of officials, the snares of false brethren; and though trials of this sort can test Catholics more thoroughly (which is the goodness of God) they cannot withdraw them from the Faith. The officials, or, as we call them, pursuivants, are troublesome everywhere to an extraordinary degree, but, especially lately, they swoop upon Catholics, ruin them, plunder them, and when possible carry them off to prison. As to the priests, if they discover any, they drag them there, and after examination, send them to the dungeons. Besides many other elsewhere, at least thirty have been captured in London since the last banishment, and thrust into prison. The rest press on with their duties, as is proper, with much praise and toil, and God giveth the increase lest they should seem to labour in vain.'

A period of relaxed persecution

During this first period of John Southworth's missionary work in his homeland, 1619 to 1624, within the reign of King James I, there was a period of relaxed persecution. This relaxation was due to political negotiations, for the King was working towards a marriage between his son, Charles, and a Catholic Princess of Spain. The King wanted peace with Spain after the long war. During these negotiations priests were not so severely treated. The last martyr of the reign, a secular Priest, also from Douay, suffered at Newcastle-under-Lyme on 30th April 1618. The King assured the Spanish Ambassador that this had been done without his knowledge, and he took steps to make his displeasure known.

In the following July the Ambassador persuaded the King to release some sixty priests from prison on condition that they left the country. The Douay Diary records the arrival of some of them; it was not long before some of them were back in England knowing full well that, if arrested, they could be executed without further trial. However a large majority of the population were still much opposed to the Papists since the Gunpowder Plot of 1605, and strongly resented any relaxation of the penal laws against Catholics.

Supporting the faith and distributing the Sacraments

John Southworth first worked in or near London. Although we have no record of his ministry we know that his main duty would be to bring the sacraments to Catholics, and to bolster the faith of those who were weakening. Some would put in a face-saving appearance at their parish church, and so become schismatic, and thus out of communion with the Catholic Church. He would try and get in touch with those in prison, and instruct those who wished to become Catholics. All these activities involved a high level of risk, of being denounced as a priest. But the Catholics in London were well organised to provide safe lodgings and to give warning of danger. The greatest danger, sad to relate, lay in 'the snares of false brethren', as the Archpriest called them; some were apostates who had sold themselves to the government, other were agents placed in the prisons.

Ministering to those in prison

John Southworth would be visiting the prisons to help both priests and lay people with the sacraments and material or monetary support. The prison system, such as it was, was very different to our ideas. To understand the 16th and 17th century prisons and what happened to priests and lay people it is important to know that the prisons were leased to gaolers or keepers who made as much money as they could out of the prisoners. Those unfortunates without money and no friends or family to help them were left in destitution; as a contemporary document tells us they would be 'lying upon the bare boards, still languishing in great need, cold and misery, almost famished and hunger-starved to death.' It was no wonder that many inmates perished of cold, hunger or disease.

Also the length of imprisonment appeared to be indeterminate, and the severity of the regulations depended largely on the political climate at the time and the disposition of one's gaolers or keepers. A typical case was that of Francis Tregian, arrested in 1577 for harbouring a priest. He spent twenty-eight years in prison in London and was only released in1606 at the request of the King of Spain. His eldest son, Francis, died in the Fleet prison in 1619, and his younger brother, Charles, died there two years later. So Catholics regularly collected funds for the relief of the poorer prisoners; no records were kept of this charitable work, but the sums raised must have been quite considerable. The priests were responsible for distributing the money and had a large share in collecting it.

In addition to the Tower of London, the state prison, there were five other prisons in London. John Southworth was eventually to experience three of them – the Clink in Southwark, the Gatehouse in Westminster and Newgate in the City. If you had money you could live quite comfortably in the Clink and likewise in the Gatehouse prison. This latter stood opposite the west door of Westminster Abbey at the top of Tothill Street, more or less where the Methodist Central Hall stands today. In 1628 a former non-catholic prisoner wrote this complaint,

> 'When I was in the Gatehouse, there were fifteen prisoners in the upper wards, whereof five were priests and all the rest papists, saving myself and two more, and upon my knowledge there is daily Mass in the house on Sundays and Holy Days, with all sorts of people from the city, money being taken for admission at the door. Weekes, the Keeper of the Gatehouse, doth falsify his trust and suffers priests to have daily intercourse.'

Newgate prison, where the Central Criminal Court now stands, was usually reserved for those likely to suffer the sentence of death; it deserved its evil reputation, for many died of its pestilential air.

False hope

During his first period of five years in London, John Southworth escaped imprisonment. Hopes were still high among Catholics that the negotiations with Spain would result in a relaxation of the penal laws. Those who harboured these thoughts were deceiving themselves, just as Catholics during Elizabeth's reign deluded themselves into thinking that a Catholic sovereign could be brought about by force of arms.

Some Catholics did not seem to have realised the rapidly increasing Puritanism of the times, nor to have understood that James, although being king, could not alter the laws or change the Oath without the consent of Parliament. He could however use his prerogative to postpone or remit the death sentence. The Ambassadors, likewise assumed wrongly that the King on his own authority, could abrogate the penal laws. In fact whenever Parliament met the demand was at once made for the stricter enforcement of the measures against papists, but there was no Parliament between June 1614 and January 1621.

Misfortune and re-inforced penal laws

During the years 1623 and 1624 misfortune seemed to dog the Catholic community. There was a crying need for a Bishop for there were thousands of Catholics deprived of the sacrament of Confirmation. When finally a Bishop, whose surname was Bishop, Bishop William Bishop, was sent to England in July 1623 to provide the benefits of Episcopal rule, he sadly died nine months later. However he did set up a Chapter of Canons under a Dean. It survives as the Old Brotherhood of the Secular Clergy. Its work today is mainly charitable, but it is an historic link with the penal days when the Chapter played an important part in preserving the Faith in England.

Later that same year some 300 Catholics met in Hunsdon House, on the third floor, near Blackfriars when the floor gave way. 90 of the congregation and 2 priests were killed. This drew attention to the number of Catholics in the capital, plus a publication by an apostate catholic which estimated that there were 261 priests in London.

Then there were grumblings about the crowds attending Masses at the Embassy chapels. By now the negotiations for a Spanish marriage for James' son Charles had fallen through and a new treaty was being sought for a marriage to the French princess Henrietta Maria, sister of King Louis XIII of France, a devout Catholic. For its approval the Commons of Parliament insisted that the laws against papists must be enforced, and a proclamation was made ordering all priests to leave the country and urging that measures should be taken to see that the children of recusants were brought up as Protestants. Once more the pursuivants got busy, and magistrates were constrained to deal with any Catholics within their jurisdiction.

Meanwhile Dr Kellison, the President of Douay College visited England for some months to try and raise funds for the Seminary which was in straitened circumstances. It may be that during this time and because of the re-enforced penal laws he had John Southworth return to Douay on 24th March 1624. He remained in the College for five months and then acted as chaplain to the English Benedictine nuns in Brussels, until he again left for the English mission in July 1625.

Lancaster 1625 - 1630

Three priests, a Benedictine, a Jesuit and a Secular share their faith in prison

On 27th March 1625 King Charles I came to the throne, and married the sister of King Louis XIII of France, Henrietta Maria, who was a devout Catholic. Also in 1625 a new Catholic Bishop was appointed, Richard Smith as Vicar Apostolic for the whole of England, Scotland and Wales, with the titular title of Bishop of Chalcedon. He resided at Turvey in Bedfordshire, at the house of Lord Montagu. Unfortunately it was not clear as to what his jurisdiction was, and the then Pope ruled that he did not have the powers of an Ordinary, or acting Bishop. This caused conflict between him and the religious orders, such as the Jesuits and Benedictines. In 1628 a warrant for his arrest was issued, and then a second, as he was 'still hidden and harboured'. Eventually he left the country in August 1631 and offered to resign. In his absence the Dean and Chapter, although not officially recognised in Rome, exercised what authority they could over the secular priests.

When John Southworth returned to England in the summer of 1625 he went to his own county, Lancashire. Here he must have met a Jesuit priest, Edmund

Arrowsmith, seven years his senior, who had returned to Lancashire from Douay in the same year in which John Southworth had entered the College. Edmund Arrowsmith came from the same county and was able to exercise his priesthood for ten years until his arrest in 1622, and then imprisonment in Lancaster castle. Fortunately for him King James wanted to make a good impression on the Spanish at that time, and, as Parliament was not sitting he ordered that all priests should be set free and Edmund Arrowsmith had another six more years of freedom when he must have got to know John Southworth, and again when they both ended up as prisoners in Lancaster castle.

John Southworth was the first to be arrested in 1627. He was condemned and given a reprieve, but not a pardon. Parliament was not then sitting. The next year, 1628 Edmund Arrowsmith was arrested, having been betrayed, and possibly John Southworth might too, have been betrayed. But Edmund Arrowsmith's trial was while Parliament was sitting, and he came before a virulently anti-catholic judge, Sir Henry Yelverton, who condemned him and insisted on the execution being carried out within forty-eight hours.

There can be little doubt that, had there been time for an appeal to King Charles, a reprieve would have been granted. There was a third priest in the Castle at that time; a Benedictine Edward Barlow. So these three priests, a

Benedictine, a Jesuit and a Secular, were able to strengthen one another in prison; all three were eventually to be martyred, but at that time, only one of them was to lay down his life.

A holy death

Bishop Challoner in 1761 in his 'British Martyrology' wrote,

'As Edmund Arrowsmith was carried through the castle-yard, there was a reverend and worthy priest, his fellow-prisoner (Mr Southworth), who had been condemned for his function a year before, and stood then reprieved, who shewed himself out of a great window. And the blessed man, who was now on his way to the hurdle, no sooner saw his face, but he lifted up his hands towards him with great humility for absolution (for this was the sign whereof they were both agreed before), and so that priest absolved the other in sight of the people. Then he was brought to the castle gates, where a Catholic gentleman embraced him straitly, and kissed him tenderly, till the High Sheriff made him be removed by force.'

Another account tells us that

'there was a gentleman who was father unto Mr Southworth, which was his fellow prisoner, who was demanded at his return from the execution what ceremonies they used at that time of his death, who did sincerely protest that in the window of his chamber he saw a most resplendent brightness, such as one as in all his life he never saw before, which did show itself from the prison unto the gallows, as if it had a glistering glow, and the sun at that time was obscured with clouds, and most part of that day likewise, which being related seemed wonderful unto us.'

From another source we know that John Southworth himself was 'very well esteemed of by Catholics', and it would have been comforting for him to have been in close touch with his own family.

A warrant and banishment

The next we hear of our martyr is of his name on a warrant in March 1630, and that he has been transferred to the Clink Prison in Southwark, London. The Clink Prison was on Bankside between Southwark Bridge and London Bridge. It was burnt down during the anti-Catholic Gordon Riots of 1780, but the site has now been made into the Clink Museum, recreating the harsh and dismal conditions that prevailed in the past. The nearest underground station is London Bridge. At the request of Queen Henrietta 16 named priests, one being John Southworth, were by the command of the Privy Council to be given into the charge of the French Ambassador for banishment and 'That if any of them shall remain in, or return into the Kingdom, that Our express will and pleasure is, That the Law should pass on every such person without further favour.'

Charles and his contrary promises

On the occasion of his marriage Charles had made two contrary promises, one to the Parliament that he would impose the penal laws in their full rigour, and at the same time he secretly promised the French King that he would do all in his power to favour and protect Catholics from those very same penal laws. Between 1629 and 1640 when he reigned without Parliament he found it easier to carry out the promises in his Marriage Agreement to grant relief to Catholics.

It is doubtful if John Southworth left the country. Being committed to the care of an Ambassador left a priest a large margin for independent action. Another priest on the same list certainly did not leave the Clink, and if John Southworth was escorted abroad he must have returned within a short time. He was certainly back in the Clink two years later, but there are indications that he had remained in England.

'The popish Royall Favourite'

William Prynne, a militant puritan and learned lawyer wrote in his book 'The Popish Royall Favourite',

'John Southworth, one of the sixteen priests released
by the King's aforecited Warrant of 11th April, to be
sent beyond the seas as was pretended; continuing a
dangerous seducer after his release, was afterwards
committed to the Clink prison by the Lords of the
Privy Council's warrant; but yet for all that had free
liberty to walk abroad at his pleasure (as most priests
during their imprisonment, had, the more safely to
seduce His Majesty's good subjects, and open Masses
in their prisons to boot).'

The old brotherhood

In that same April we also find John Southworth's name
in a document in the archives of the Old Brotherhood.
This organisation was formed of Catholic priests who did
their best to organise and help their fellow priests in the
very difficult and dangerous missionary situation in
which they found themselves. The document reads as
follows, 'We whose names are here underwritten do
freely give to the body of the English Clergy the sum of
two hundred pounds sterling apiece, reserving only to
ourselves the rent-charge thereof during our natural lives
and a year after to be applied for the benefit of our souls
by the Dean and Chapter.' John Southworth's name was
among those who made this loan, a considerable sum in
those days. Although we know nothing of his financial
situation the making of this loan suggests that he or his

family were not without funds to alleviate his times in prison. We also discover that he was well enough off to have a man-servant. This from an inscription in a book, 'Ex dono John Southworth who died a Martir for the Catholick Faith. June 28th, 1654 – to his servant Jo. Lillie.' Many of the priests, however, had no private means, and they depended for their maintenance on the generosity of the Catholic laity, and, as here shown, on that of their more fortunate brethren.

London 1630 - 1635

A Catholic Queen and an absent bishop

John Southworth's arrival at the Clink from Lancaster was the beginning of a ministry of twenty-five years in London. How many of those years were spent in prison it is impossible to estimate as the necessary records do not exist; up to the outbreak of the civil war, he was certainly more often in prison than out. Whether in prison or out, John Southworth was able to keep in touch with his fellow priests in London.

Then came a period of twelve years of which we know practically nothing. From 1629 to 1640 the King ruled without Parliament; no priest was sent to the gallows during those years. This less severe treatment was in part due to the Catholic Queen. Her two chapels, one at St Jame's, the other at Somerset House, were thronged at Mass. Unfortunately the King and his Archbishop, William Laud, and the Papal Agents appointed to the Queen seem to have been unaware of the rapidly increasing strength of Puritan feeling in the country.

In 1631 the Vicar Apostolic, Bishop Richard Smith, due to the many problems he had encountered had retired to France, leaving the Catholic Church in England without a leader. The subsequent disputes about the extent of his authority left the Chapter to do what it could to maintain the organisation in working order, but the absence of the Bishop was a grave handicap and the Regulars, especially the Jesuits, were accused by the Seculars of opposing the appointment of a Bishop. In July 1632 twenty-four priests wrote to the Bishop as they had heard rumours that he was going to resign; they begged him not to do so but to return to them.

The second document, a month later, was a petition to the Pope; this was signed by thirty-nine priests. After describing the difficulties created by the absence of a Bishop, they asked that Bishop Smith should be sent back to them with the full authority needed to settle the unfortunate disputes that divided the clergy.

We find John Southworth's name on both these lists, and also named in the list of priests in the Clink in 1632, kept by the Old Brotherhood. In 1635 he is listed by a pursuivant as condemned, referring back to his condemnation at Lancaster in 1627. This sentence was in abeyance, but he had not been pardoned and the pursuivants were not allowing this to be forgotten.

Plague-stricken Westminster
1636 - 1640

Papist poverty and alms distribution

John Southworth though technically a prisoner was most of the time out on parole, working amongst the desperately poor Catholics that crowded the narrow 'courts' and 'passages' behind streets so appallingly noxious that it is difficult for us to imagine. Two areas were notorious for papists; the warren of back alleys in the parish of St Giles, Holborn, and the west end of the parish of St Margaret's, Westminster, both slums. Huddled together in indescribable conditions of overcrowding, hunger and near nakedness they did not, as papists, qualify for poor relief, such as it was. They depended on the bounty of the Queen and the Catholic laity of means. These alms were distributed by a small band of devoted priests, most of them prisoners out on parole as was John Southworth.

Epidemics

Almost every summer there was an epidemic that carried off young and old. For several years it amounted to a plague and claimed thousands of victims each week. In

1626 over thirty five thousand deaths were reported, and in 1636 a lesser number of twelve thousand deaths were reported, though there must have been many more due to the imperfect way of collecting statistics in those days. Those who could afford it moved out to the country and it was always the poor who were forced to remain. The only known hygienic measures were to lock up the contaminated in their crowded hovels. These houses were marked with a cross and nobody was allowed to visit them. Such was the scene and the nature of John's apostolate till he was called upon to make the extreme sacrifice of his life.

Two priests among the plague stricken
- Henry Morse and John Southworth

The names of two priests, Henry Morse a Jesuit and that of John Southworth who both toiled among the plague stricken, have been preserved for us because their activities aroused the animosity of the Anglican clergy who lodged complaints with the Privy Council. These two priests were chosen to organise the work and collect alms. Eighteen years before Henry Morse had been at Douay and most probably knew John Southworth there, but he had then gone on to Rome where he joined the Jesuits.

When the plague broke out he was working round about St Giles-in-the-Fields, one of the most ill-famed parts of London, known as 'the rookery'. John Southworth was at work in a similar haunt of wretchedness, the part between Westminster Abbey and Whitehall. One of the alleys being appropriately called Thieving Lane. His area also stretched south of the Abbey including the present Tothill Street. Two hundred years later, Cardinal Wiseman would still be able to describe this area as 'a labyrinth of alleys and slums, a nest of ignorance, vice, depravity, and crime, as well as of squalor and disease; whose atmosphere is typhus, whose ventilation is cholera.' He would no doubt have visited the Westminster Pest House, or hospital for plague victims, in the angle now made by Regency Street with Vauxhall Bridge Road, and the new prison built in 1618 which stood on the present site of Westminster Cathedral.

A disagreement

The two priests didn't always agree as to the way they administered the sacraments as can be seen from this extract from one of the Annual Letters of the Jesuits:

'Father Morse, in the first days of his attendance on the sick, whether overpowered at the outset by the formidable and noxious symptoms of the disease, or anxious to leave none of the daily increasing number of patients without the necessary help, or else deeming it prudent to avoid a less necessary danger, satisfied himself with administering the Sacraments of Penance

and of the Blessed Eucharist, and omitted that of
Extreme Unction. His secular coadjutor [John
Southworth] hearing of this omission, began to
complain of what he called the unworthy timidity of his
fellow-labourer. But Father Morse, hearing of this
report, submitted to the charge with religious humility,
and, blaming none but himself, at once discarded his
apprehensions and administered to the infected all the
aids of religion.'

After this the two priests worked in harmony. Indeed when
John Southworth was struck down by illness and confined
to the Gatehouse, Henry Morse also visited Westminster
on his behalf, and likewise when Henry Morse succumbed
to illness John Southworth cared for the St Giles area as
well as his own.

Deathbed reconciliation - an act of treason!

It is not surprising that as John visited the sick and the
dying, the grief stricken and the unburied dead, he made
no distinction between Catholics and others. They were
near enough to Catholic days to have the traditions of
how a Christian should die. Many had lapsed through
ignorance or timidity and sought a deathbed
reconciliation. And each act of reconciliation was an act
of treason! John, already a priest condemned, was
committing a capital offence in every hovel he entered.

Soon the sub-curate (note his rank), Robert White, of St Margaret's, Westminster, was making a complaint to the Archbishop of Canterbury, in August 1636. Again we know of this through the writings of William Prynne, a militant puritan who gathered in one volume in 1643, 'The Popish Royall Favourite', all the evidence of concessions made to Papists by King Charles I. John Southworth is accused that under the pretence of distributing Alms, sent from Priests in Somerset House, where Queen Henrietta had a Catholic Chapel, he would persuade people to change their religion at the point of death to become Romish-Catholic and receive the Sacraments according to the Church of Rome. He is called a dangerous seducer, persuading Catholics to keep away from their parish churches and refuse the oath of allegiance, and, secondly, that he was making converts.

An appeal

As a result of the complaint John Southworth was more closely confined in the Gatehouse. But this did not prevent him from joining with Henry Morse, who was at liberty, in making an appeal to Catholics for more funds in aid of the plague victims, in their words 'to procure due relief for the poor Catholics of London'.

We have a copy of this appeal signed, and dated 6th October 1636, by Henry Morse and John Southworth and endorsed by the Vicar General of the London District.

George Muskett, and George Gage, his successor, which was printed and addressed 'To the Catholics of England'. It described the desperate plight of their fellow co-religionists,

> 'shut up within the bare walls of a poor chamber, having not wherewithal to allay the rage of hunger, nor scarcely to cover nakedness. There are others, who for the space of three days together have not got a morsel of bread to put into their mouths. At this present there are about fifty several families, which are visited and shut up, brought to the brink of despair'.

The response was generous. The Queen herself contributed 500 gold crowns, roughly about 10,000 pounds in today's money, and continued to support the fund. But complaints were made by the Rector of St Giles to the Privy Council and Henry Morse was arrested and sent to Newgate to be condemned in April 1637, but the sentence was not passed due to the intercession of George Con, the papal agent to the Queen. Eventually he was re-arrested and the condemnation put into effect. He was executed at Tyburn 1st February 1645.

A petition to the Queen

John Southworth was more fortunate. In 1637 he wrote a petition in his own hand, a copy of which we still have, directly to the Queen to be released from his close confinement in the Gatehouse prison. This petition was granted, much to the annoyance of the puritan party, of whose members found themselves 'most grievously censured in the Star Chamber, and most barbarously pilloried, deprived of their ears, stigmatised'. However, from the records, John Southworth was in prison during most of the period 1627 to 1640 with two or three brief intervals of freedom. There may well have been about 200 priests at work in or near London at that time; some of their names appear once or twice without any particulars to distinguish one from another. But John Southworth's name appears the greatest number of times. No doubt that is why he was described by the pursuivants as a 'great seducer'. That seems to have been his reputation.

It means that his success in making converts and in persuading Catholics to persevere in their faith was so notable that the authorities became alarmed about his activities. Bribes to prison keepers helped him, but his life was spared by the influence of the Queen and by the King's reluctance to allow the law against priests to be carried out to the full. Sir Francis Windebank, Secretary of State was a good friend to Catholics. In July of 1640 he signed a warrant for John Southworth to be set at liberty. He believed that the breach between Rome and England would be repaired if only both Puritans and Jesuits could be got out of the way! He was denounced at the Long Parliament for having stopped the proceedings against 74 recusants and to have released as many as 64 priests in one year.

But then in December 1640 there is a record of John Southworth as being moved from the Clink Prison to the Gatehouse Prison. But this is the last official record we have from 1640 until his arrest in 1654. So from the accession of Charles I to the throne in 1625 until 1640 there was only one priest and one layman executed for their religion. But in 1640 the Puritan Long Parliament met and renewed the persecution. There was a Royal Proclamation to banish Jesuits, priests and seminarists under penalty of death. From 1640 until the end of Charles' reign in 1649 there were a total of 20 executions of priests and laymen.

Old Bailey 1640 - 1654

Catholics in high places flee

By the end of 1640 King Charles I had lost effective control of the country and the power was in the hands of a Puritan Government. Soon Secretary Windebank, who had proved such a good friend to priests, was summoned before the Council to be reprimanded, and he fled to France and there became a Catholic. Later Queen Henrietta followed him and Catholics were deprived of their protectors in high places.

The civil war - A losing side

Soon came the civil war, with the Catholics on the losing side, the King then executed, and the Cromwellian regime. After more than twenty years almost free of martyrs, innocent blood began to flow again in 1641. There were 22 victims before the end of 1645. During all this time John Southworth is scarcely heard of. He was doubtless in and out of prison and still ministering to his beloved poor. Meanwhile the new Secretary of State, Windebank's successor, warned King Charles that one of the causes of his unpopularity was his toleration of Catholics. So in York, 1642, he signed the death warrants of John Lockwood (aged 81) and Edward Catherick, both secular priests.

The Civil war between King Charles and Oliver Cromwell begins in 1642. It has been estimated that two out of every five of the royalist officers killed during the war were Catholics. At the start of the war London was divided in its support and throughout the war there were royalists living in London or nearby. But on 15th May 1643 Parliament ordered the Mayor to expel all recusants and their wives, but the order could not be carried out in full. The authorities were too much preoccupied with military matters to spend time on hunting down priests.

House priests could work in comparative safety in those troubled times. But laws against Catholics were increased as with a new oath imposed in 1643 in which a Catholic had to reject papal supremacy and the doctrines of transubstantiation and purgatory. Catholic Royalists with property suffered heavily, and those who took up arms had their lands confiscated. We do not know how long John Southworth remained in the Gatehouse prison after 1640.

John Southworth's arrest

The next we hear of him is of his arrest in 1654 from lodgings in Westminster. A letter from the Venetian Secretary in London written to the Venetian Ambassador in Paris, dated 9th July 1654, tells of 'an English priest found in his bed chamber with all the requisites for the celebration of Mass, to which he intrepidly owned, they compelled him to get up and carried him off prisoner.' The court records give the date of his arrest as 19th June. His arrest was made upon the information of one Jefferies, a pursuivant, whom John Southworth 'had in fee', in other words was paying Jefferies bribery monies to preserve his freedom.

The arresting officer was Colonel Worsley, one of Cromwell's younger and most puritanical officers. The indictment was 'that he had been made and ordained a Priest by authority derived and pretended from the See of Rome and was resident in the Commonwealth contrary to the laws and statutes of England'.

John Southworth's trial - a magistrate drowned in tears

The Delivery Register of Newgate records that he was committed for trial on 21st June and that he was tried at the Old Bailey on 24th June. Here according to the Westminster Archives, 'he confessed himself a priest, and a condemned man many years since. On Monday the 26th he was again called to the bar again'. From Bishop Challoner, writing in 1687 we learn that

> 'his judges did their utmost to preserve his life, and to prevent the execution against him of those laws upon which he stood indicted; for they did for many hours suspend the recording of his confession, making it their endeavour to prevail with him to plead "Not Guilty" to

the indictment. They pressed him to this in the public court, assuring him that if he would so plead his life would be safe, and that they had no evidence which could prove him to be a priest. And when the old man would not be drawn to deny himself to be a priest, taking it to be a denying of his religion, and that the court was compelled to give judgment against him, the magistrate who gave the sentence was so drowned in tears upon that sad occasion, that it was long before he could pronounce the sentence which the law compelled'.

Following the pronouncement of the death sentence on him John Southworth was given leave to say a few words to the court, which he did; and falling on his knees said: 'O Lord God, I humbly thank thee, who hath made me worthy to suffer for Thy sake.' Then standing up, he said to the court: 'I thank you for what you have done, and for your civilities to me, and I pray God to give you His holy grace, that you and all this nation may be converted to the true Roman, Catholic and Apostolic Faith, and remain in heaven for ever with Jesus Christ in glory.' The Recorder said: 'Sir, we thank you, and will join you in the latter part.'

Several ambassadors interceded with Cromwell, notably the French and Portuguese, and the Spanish Ambassador who bought his body off the hangman for forty shillings. The Venetian Secretary wrote, 'When Cromwell was informed of this incident he seemed moved and averse from such cruelty, expressing himself, possibly from deceit or shrewdness, as opposed to violence in matters of religion and in favour of liberty of conscience for all, yet he was obliged to approve the deed and sanction this sacrifice to the law of the land'.

The fact is that no priest was put to death between 1654 and 1678. It was possibly only due to the Oates Plot in the reign of Charles II that further martyrdoms took place. However John Southworth was the last secular priest to suffer at Tyburn.

Tyburn 28th June 1654

The last sermon at the gallows

On the 28th June 1654 John Southworth was dragged on a hurdle from Newgate prison, through Holborn and so to Tyburn gallows near the spot where Marble Arch now stands. A brass plaque in the road marks the actual site of the gallows. Although it was a stormy and rainy day several thousand people and a great number of coaches and horsemen had gathered to witness this execution of nine men and a woman. Five of these were guilty of coining, in other words making counterfeit coinage, a treasonable offence, and, like the priest, their bodies were to be quartered.

It was usual to reserve the priest as the last victim, and John was allowed to speak to the crowd, his last sermon; he was clothed in a priest's gown, and had a four-cornered cap. We are fortunate to have five contemporary manuscript versions of his speech, one made by an unknown priest who stood near the gallows for the purpose of giving that final Absolution.

'Good people, I was born in Lancashire. This is the third time I have been apprehended, and now being to die, I would gladly witness and profess openly my faith for which I suffer. And though my time be short, yet what I shall be deficient in words I hope I shall supply with my blood, which I will most willingly spend to the last drop for my faith. Neither my coming into England, nor practice in England, was to act anything against the secular government. Hither I was sent by my lawful superiors to teach Christ's faith, not to meddle with any temporal affairs. Christ sent His apostles; His apostles, their successors; and their successors me. I did what I was commanded by them, who had power to command me, being ever taught that I ought to obey them in matters ecclesiastical, and my temporal governors in business only temporal.

I never acted nor thought any hurt against the present Protector (Oliver Cromwell). I had only a care to do my own obligation and discharge my own duty in saving my own and other men's souls. This, and only this, according to my poor abilities I laboured to perform. I had commission to do it from him to whom our Saviour in his predecessor St Peter, gave power to send others to propagate His faith. This is that for which I die, O holy cause! and not for any treason against the laws.

My faith and obedience to my superiors is all the treason charged against me; nay, I die for Christ's law, which no human law, by whomsoever made, ought to withstand or contradict. The law of Christ commanded me to obey these superiors and this Church, saying, whoever hears them hears Himself. This Church, these superiors of it I obeyed, and for obeying, die. This lesson I have heretofore in my lifetime desired to learn; this lesson I come here to put in practice by dying, being taught it by our Blessed Saviour, both by precept and example. Himself said, "He that will be My disciple, let him take up his cross and follow Me." Himself exemplary, practised what He had recommended to others. To follow His holy doctrine and imitate His holy death, I willingly suffer at present; this gallows (looking up) I look on as His cross, which I gladly take to follow my dear Saviour.

My faith is my crime, the performance of my duty the occasion of my condemnation. I confess I am a great sinner; against God I have offended, but am innocent of any sin against man, I mean the Commonwealth and the present Government. How justly then I die, let them look to who have condemned me. It is sufficient for me that it is God's will; I plead not for myself (I came hither to suffer) but for you poor persecuted Catholics whom I leave behind me.

Heretofore liberty of conscience was pretended as a cause of war; and it was held a reasonable proposition that all the natives should enjoy it, who should be found to behave themselves as obedient and true subjects. This being so, why should their conscientious acting and governing themselves, according to the faith received from their ancestors, involve them more than all the rest in an universal guilt? - which conscientiousness is the very reason that clears others and renders them innocent.

It has pleased God to take the sword out of the King's hand and put it in the Protector's. Let him remember that he is to administer justice indifferently and without exception of persons. For there is no exception of persons with God whom we ought to resemble. If any Catholics work against the present Government, let them suffer; but why should the rest who are guiltless (unless conscience be their guilt) be made partakers in a promiscuous punishment with the greatest malefactors? The first rebellion was of the angels; the guilty were cast into hell, the innocent remained partakers of the heavenly blessings.'

Here he was interrupted by some officers wanting him to make haste. 'He then requested all present that were Catholics to pray for him and with him. After which, with hands raised up to heaven and eyes (after a short prayer in silence) gently shut, he waited for the moment of execution, which immediately followed, and which he suffered with unmoved quietness, delivering his soul most blessedly into the hands of his most loving God, who died for him, and for whose sake he died'.

A barbarous execution

The execution by hanging is described by the Venetian Secretary as follows, 'Then in a fashion worse than barbarous, when he was only half dead, the executioner cut out his heart and entrails and threw them into a fire kindled for the purpose, the body being quartered, one for each of the quarters of the city. Such is the inhuman cruelty used towards the English Catholic religious. When discovered they can hope for no pardon. To the last he displayed the greatest cheerfulness, determination and constancy, and at the point of death he boldly thanked the Almighty for permitting him to die for his faith'.

A vocation

In the crowd was a young royalist soldier, twenty three years of age. He recorded that on witnessing the execution of the most blessed martyr, John Southworth, he resolved to go to Rome, in order, as far as he could, to render some service, however unworthy, to Holy Church. He entered the English College, Rome, on 9th September 1654; he became a Jesuit and served on the mission at Kelvedon, Essex, where he died in 1679.

Return to Douay - 1655

Bribing the hangman and taking the body out of the country

The Venetian Secretary had been misinformed when he reported that the quarters of the martyr had been put up in four places in the City. That was required by law, but it was sometimes possible for relatives or friends to bribe the hangman so that they could give the remains a seemly burial. Richard Symonds a royalist and antiquary wrote in his notebook that the Spanish Ambassador bought the remains from the hangman for forty shillings, two pounds sterling in today's currency. The Ambassador, Alonzo de Cardenas, was no doubt acting on behalf of some leading English Catholics who also would make arrangements for the embalmment.

This was carried out by a surgeon, James Clark, of whom nothing more is known. His name is preserved on a piece of paper which was attached to a relic now at Westminster Cathedral; the relic was a bone out of the spine. The faded wording reads: 'This bone taken out of ye neck of Mr South ? (rest of the name illegible) who suffered under Oliver Cromwell as a Catholic Priest or Clergyman, was given me by Mr James Clark,

Chirurgeon, who embalmed ye body'. Despite the
illegibility of the name the reference to Oliver Cromwell
is decisive as the only other martyr under the
Commonwealth was the Jesuit priest, Peter Wright, who
suffered at Tyburn in 1651.

The good offices of the Spanish Ambassador were no
doubt called upon to help solve the problems of
conveying the body across the Channel to France. This
was not done until nearly a year later, in June 1655. It
would have been too dangerous for any English Catholic
to have attempted to take the body out of the country. We
do not know where the body was kept during this time.

Bishop Challoner writes in 1741 in his Memoirs of
Missionary Priests, 'Mr Southworth's body was sent over
to the English College of Douay by one of the illustrious
family of Howards of Norfolk, and deposited in the
church near St Augustine's altar'. And this was its
position in Challoner's own day; he entered Douay in
1705, and the President of the College at that time was Dr
Edward Paston who had been a boy at the College when
John Southworth was martyred, and no doubt he would
recall in later years the reception of the body in 1655; it
must have been a great day in the history of the College.

The then President of the College, Dr George Leyburn
wrote to their Cardinal Protector in Rome, Francesco
Barberini, describing the devotion of the people of Douai.
They have a 'seemingly inborn attraction towards Christ's

holy heroes who have sealed their Catholic and Apostolic faith with their blood, that constantly, day by day, they are kneeling at the tomb, pouring out their prayers'.

A seeming miracle

A seeming miracle occured the following year, 1656, when a fifteen year old boy, a member of the Howard family which enabled the martyr's body to be enshrined at Douay College, fell terribly ill of a fever and the doctors despaired of his life with him, not sleeping, or eating for four or five days – 'there is not the least hope'. Yet after fervent prayer and letting him lay his head on the cushion that supported the martyr's head there was, in the word of one of the witnesses, 'a miraculous recovery of a man only not quite dead'.

It seems that the body of John Southworth was not buried. Bishop Challoner writes of it being near St Augustine's altar in the College Chapel, while Dr Leyburn, the President of the College in 1656 wrote of a tomb.

The French Revolution; the body hidden in a kiln

The French Revolution in the 1790s created the need for removing the body to a secret place of security. The Revolution as it progressed became increasingly anti-Catholic. The Cathedral of Paris, Notre Dame, was desecrated, with a pagan idol placed in it. King Louis

XVI was executed on 21st January 1793, and with the declaration of war against England the College was in an extremely vulnerable position. The National Guards took possession of the College and all those in residence become prisoners.

The College had many treasures – Church plate, relics of St Thomas of Canterbury, the biretta of St Charles Borromeo, and of course the body of John Southworth. All of these were buried by the Priests and students and the whereabouts of the varied items noted. So Bishop Douglas writes, 'Mr Southworth's body in the kilns exactly six feet deep.' 4th May 1793. Father Thomas Stout, one of the priests involved with the burial, drew a rough diagram. The kilns were the malt kilns used for making the College beer in the small brewery. The beer made was called 'small beer' and would have been the daily beverage in those days at their meals. Tea and coffee were so highly priced that they were luxury goods enjoyed only by the wealthy.

In August 1793 all the College members were expelled from the College but kept in France under surveillance until early in 1795 negotiations led to their release and they landed at Dover on 2nd March. One of the College priests brought with him part of the tape that had been tied round the leaden coffin in which is enclosed the body of John Southworth. There is no record of when the body was placed in its leaden shell, but this hermetically sealed metal coffin would clearly have protected the remains for the one hundred and thirty four years that it remained buried.

A search

It wasn't till seventy years later in 1863 when the Catholic hierarchy had been restored that Cardinal Wiseman got the necessary authority for a search to be made. In 1834 the College buildings became the property of the French army and were turned into barracks. So when the searchers arrived at Douai, led by Mgr Searle, they were baffled by some of the changes made in the buildings and even with the rough sketch map they could only find some of the plate. They were not able to find the box of relics nor the leaden coffin buried in the kiln-house, although they must have been very close to them. So the first search came to an end.

Return to Westminster - 1930

Uncovering the coffin

In 1893 Bishop Bernard Wall wrote in his 'History of St
Edmund's College' that even if Mgr Searle had known
exactly where to look it is more than doubtful whether
anything would have been left of the relics after seventy-
five years under ground. It is probable that nothing more
would have been done had it not been for plans for town
development at Douai in 1923. This involved the
demolition of the College buildings which were no long
needed as a barracks. A new road was to be made
diagonally across the site; part of the ground was to be
levelled as an open space and the rest sold for private
building. The scheme was not carried out until 1926, and
in September the old College buildings were demolished.

Providentially, on the one plot of ground of the college
site where the new owner wanted a cellar dug the
workmen uncovered a leaden coffin, or shell, shaped in
the form of a body. It was removed to the local morgue,
and thoroughly cleaned but no inscription was found on
the coffin. The shell was then opened; inside was a body
tightly swathed in linen bands. Water had seeped through
a small hole and had done some damage.

Also discovered nearby was the box containing a portion of the hair shirt of St Thomas Becket of Canterbury and the red biretta of St Charles Borromeo. Sadly the workman threw away what he thought was a piece of old cloth and the relic of St Thomas was irretrievably lost. Fortunately the three pieces of St Charles' biretta were in fair condition and were saved; this relic is now kept at St Edmund's College, Ware, Herts.

Hung, drawn and quartered - a martyrs body

A close examination of the body was carried out by the Director of the Institute of Legal Medicine at Lille. The following is a description of what was observed: the body had kept its general form quite well. The head was found to be in a good state of preservation with a slight moustache and beard in the style of Cardinal Richelieu, of chestnut colour; the orbs of the eyes were empty and the ears had been severed. The crown of the head had been carefully sawn off and the brain removed, the cavity filled with wads of embalming material. The head was sewn to the trunk with careful stitching.

Of the missing members, hands, ears and crown of the head, there was no trace in the coffin, nor did a painstaking search reveal any document or object of any kind which might have given a clue to the identity of the body or the date of its burial.

X-ray photographs of the body revealed beyond any doubt that the body had been quartered. The head had been cut off probably with an axe or chopper, and both legs had similarly been severed: there was a violent cut through the spinal column, and the pelvis was broken in two. It was easy to see where the quarters had been sewn together. The body shows that the martyr suffered the full penalty implied by being 'hanged, drawn, and quartered'.

It was known that the martyr's body had been embalmed and taken to Douai in 1655, and that in 1793 it had been taken from the Chapel and buried in as safe a place as could be used at a time of danger. There was no record of any other embalmed body having been taken to the College.

Fortunately the plan made by Fr Stout at the time of the burial was re-discovered at Douai Abbey, Woolhampton. Cardinal Bourne sent Fr Albert Purdie as his representative to Douai, and after studying Fr Stout's plan he came to the conclusion that 'the spot shown by Fr Stout is identical with the spot where the body and relics were actually found on July 15-16, 1927.' After the necessary formalities on December 20th 1927, the body of St John Southworth was handed over to Fr Purdie, intact except for the left clavicle bone and the right forearm which were left at Douai at the request of the Archbishop of Cambrai as a precious memorial of the great English College which for three hundred years had acted as a beacon of Faith throughout the Catholic world.

The body returns home - beatification
and canonisation

The body was then taken to St Edmund's College, Ware, which with Ushaw College, Durham, is the lineal descendant of the Douay Seminary on English soil. For three years his body rested in the Douay Room at St Edmund's. Then, after the official post-mortem required by Canon Law was carried out, on 15th December 1929, the centenary year of Catholic Emancipation, 136 English and Welsh martyrs were beatified by the solemn decree of the Holy Father, Pope Pius XI; among them being John Southworth.

Then on the 1st May 1930 John Southworth arrived back to his original parish of Westminster re-embalmed and carried in state within a glass and bronze feretory covered with a silken pall. The bearers were 8 priests – 2 Seculars, 2 Benedictines, 2 Franciscans, and 2 Jesuits. At the head of the procession were the men of the Guild of the Blessed Sacrament, then the choir, the College of Cathedral Chaplains, the members of the Chapter, the Canons of the Diocese, 8 Bishops and 2 Archbishops. Behind the feretory came the Archbishop, Cardinal Francis Bourne. At the end of the ceremony the feretory was solemnly placed in the Chapel of St George and the English Martyrs, where it remains to this day.

In 1955 the feretory was opened, the body clothed in more becoming vestments, the discoloured face covered with a silver mask, and the missing hands replaced in silver. He now wears a four cornered cap, as mentioned by one who saw the execution.

Finally on 25th October 1970 John Southworth was canonised as a Saint with 39 English and Welsh fellow martyrs, Priests, Religious, and lay people, by his holiness Pope Paul VI in St Peter's Basilica, Rome. St Peter's was filled to overflowing that day with an English speaking congregation, and it was a wonderful and never to be forgotten occasion to hear such favourite hymns as 'Full in the panting heart of Rome' sung with such fervour, right there 'Beneath the apostle's crowning dome', to honour our forebears and the successor of St Peter.

Westminster Cathedral is singularly blessed in having its own Parish Priest, of over twenty years standing, as a martyr saint. I know of no other church with such a claim to fame. Every day people pray before his mortal remains and his feast day is kept as a Solemnity in the Cathedral on 27th June, the eve of the anniversary of his martyrdom in 1654.

As we look at the remains of our martyr saint in his red vestments and four-cornered black cap it is easy to visualise him as he was in the days of his flesh more than three centuries ago when he used to slip out of the Gatehouse prison at dusk into the noisome alleys and yards of Westminster, the very streets and pavements we tread today, to bring comfort to the sick and to fortify the faithful with the Sacraments.

Prayers

Prayer to Saint John Southworth

Almighty God,

You made your Church grow
through the missionary zeal and apostolic work
of Saint John Southworth.
By the help of his prayers
give your Church continued growth
and an increase among its people
of holiness and faith.
We make this prayer
through our Lord
Jesus Christ your Son
who lives and reigns with you
and the Holy Spirit,
one God
for ever and ever.
Amen.

Prayer for England

In the Middle Ages, England was known as Our Lady's Dowry, because there were more churches dedicated to Mary than to any other title.

This prayer, in its original form written by Cardinal Merry del Val, has traditionally been said at Benediction. It is a prayer for the unity of the Church in England.

O Blessed Virgin Mary, Mother of God, and our most gentle queen and mother, look down in mercy upon England, your dowry, and upon us all who greatly hope and trust in you. By you it was that Jesus, our Saviour and our hope, was given to the world; and he has given you to us that we may hope still more.

Plead for us your children, whom you received and accepted at the foot of the cross, O mother of sorrows. Pray for our separated brethren, that in the one true fold of Christ, we may all be united under the care of Pope N., the chief shepherd of Christ's flock. Pray for us all, dear mother, that by faith, and fruitful in good works, we may all deserve to see and praise God, together with you in our heavenly home.